NEIL A. KJOS
PIANO LIBRARY

D0904560

LEVEL TEN

PIANO REPERTOIRE

SELECTED & EDITED BY

Keith Snell

Romantic & 20th Century

THE NEIL A. KJOS PIANO LIBRARY

The **Neil A. Kjos Piano Library** is a comprehensive series of piano music in a wide variety of musical styles. The library is divided into eleven levels and will provide students with a complete performance experience in both solo and ensemble music. Teachers will find the carefully graded levels appropriate when choosing repertoire for evaluations, auditions, festivals, and examinations. Included in the **Neil A. Kjos Piano Library:**

Preparatory Level - Level Ten

Fundamentals of Piano Theory
Piano Repertoire: Baroque & Classical
Piano Repertoire: Romantic & 20th Century
Piano Repertoire: Etudes
Scale Skills
Essential Piano Repertoire
Music of the 21st Century
New Age Piano
Jazz Piano
One Piano Four Hands
Music for Christmas

PREFACE

Piano Repertoire: Romantic & 20th Century from the **Neil A. Kjos Piano Library** provides piano students with carefully chosen collections of piano music from the 19th and 20th centuries. Each volume contains an ample selection of music featuring a large assortment of composers and styles. The appropriately graded levels ensure steady and thorough progress as pianists advance in their study of Romantic and 20th Century keyboard literature.

Compact disc recordings are available for each volume in the *Piano Repertoire* series. Recorded by pianist Diane Hidy, the interpretations follow the editions closely as practical examples for students. Each CD includes all three volumes from the *Piano Repertoire* series at each level: *Baroque & Classical*, *Romantic & 20th Century*, and *Etudes*.*

*Preparatory and Level One are included on one CD.

CONTENTS

ISBN 0-8497-6247-2

©1997 Neil A. Kjos Music Company, 4380 Jutland Drive, San Diego, California 92117
International copyright secured. All rights reserved. Printed in U.S.A.
Warning! These arrangements are protected by copyright law. To copy or reproduce them by any method is an infringement of the copyright law. Anyone who reproduces copyrighted matter is subject to substantial penalties and assessments for each infringement.

Impromptu
Op. 90, No. 4

Franz Schubert
(1797-1828)

© 1997 Neil A. Kjos Music Company, 4380 Jutland Drive, San Diego, California, 92117.

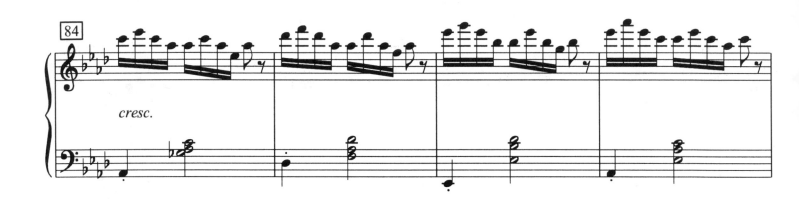

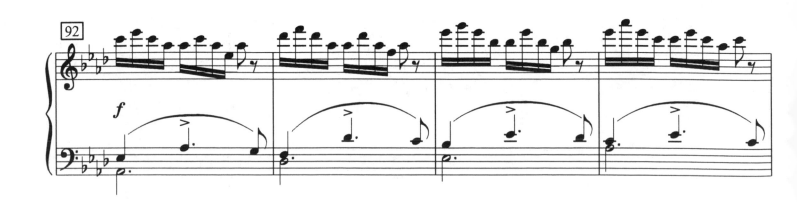

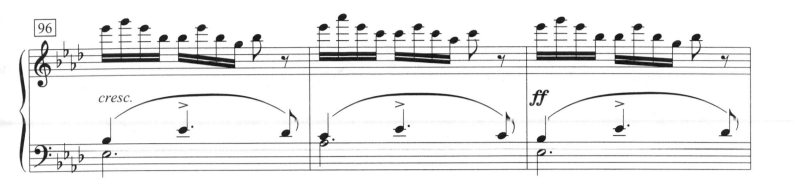

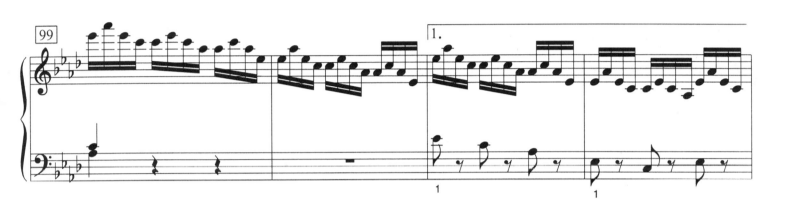

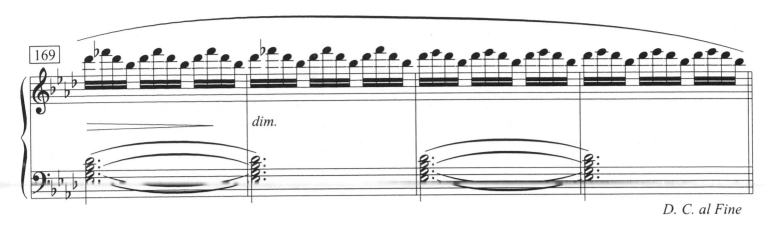

D. C. al Fine

Scherzo

Op. 16, No. 2

Felix Mendelssohn
(1809-1847)

* No pedal change in original edition.

Grillen

Whims

Op. 12, No. 4

Robert Schumann
(1810-1856)

© 1997 Neil A. Kjos Music Company, 4380 Jutland Drive, San Diego, California, 92117.

20

© 1997 Neil A. Kjos Music Company, 4380 Jutland Drive, San Diego, California, 92117.

Nocturne

Op. 55, No. 1

Frederic Chopin
(1810-1849)

© 1997 Neil A. Kjos Music Company, 4380 Jutland Drive, San Diego, California, 92117.

Waltz

Op. Post.

Frederic Chopin
(1810-1849)

© 1997 Neil A. Kjos Music Company, 4380 Jutland Drive, San Diego, California, 92117.

Fantasie-Impromptu

Op. 66

Frederic Chopin
(1810-1849)

© 1997 Neil A. Kjos Music Company, 4380 Jutland Drive, San Diego, California, 92117.

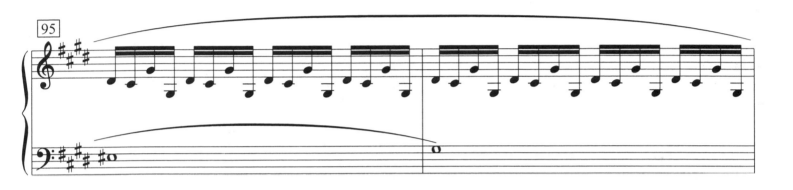

Rhapsody

Op. 79, No. 2

Johannes Brahms
(1833-1897)

Molto passionato, ma non troppo allegro

© 1997 Neil A. Kjos Music Company, 4380 Jutland Drive, San Diego, California, 92117.

Clair de Lune 8-9

From *Suite Bergamasque*

Claude Debussy
(1862 -1918)

Andante trés expressif

© 1997 Neil A. Kjos Music Company, 4380 Jutland Drive, San Diego, California, 92117.

GP630

Tempo rubato

peu   a   peu   cresc.   et   animé

r. h.

pp

dim.   molto

8va

En animant

più cresc.

f

dim.

Prelude

Op. 11, No. 1

Anatoli Liadov
(1855 -1914)

©1997 Neil A. Kjos Music Company, 4380 Jutland Drive, San Diego, California, 92117

Preludium

Op. 10, No. 1

Largamente con Energia
With Energy and Breadth

Edward MacDowell
(1860-1908)

© 1997 Neil A. Kjos Music Company, 4380 Jutland Drive, San Diego, California, 92117.

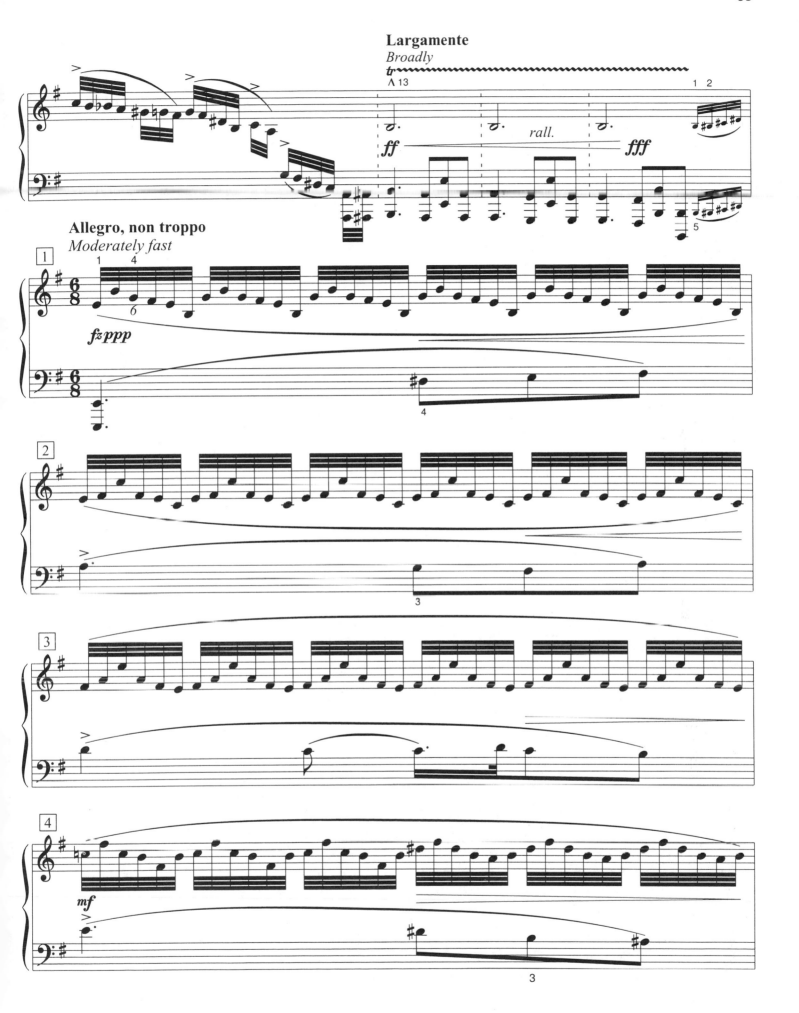

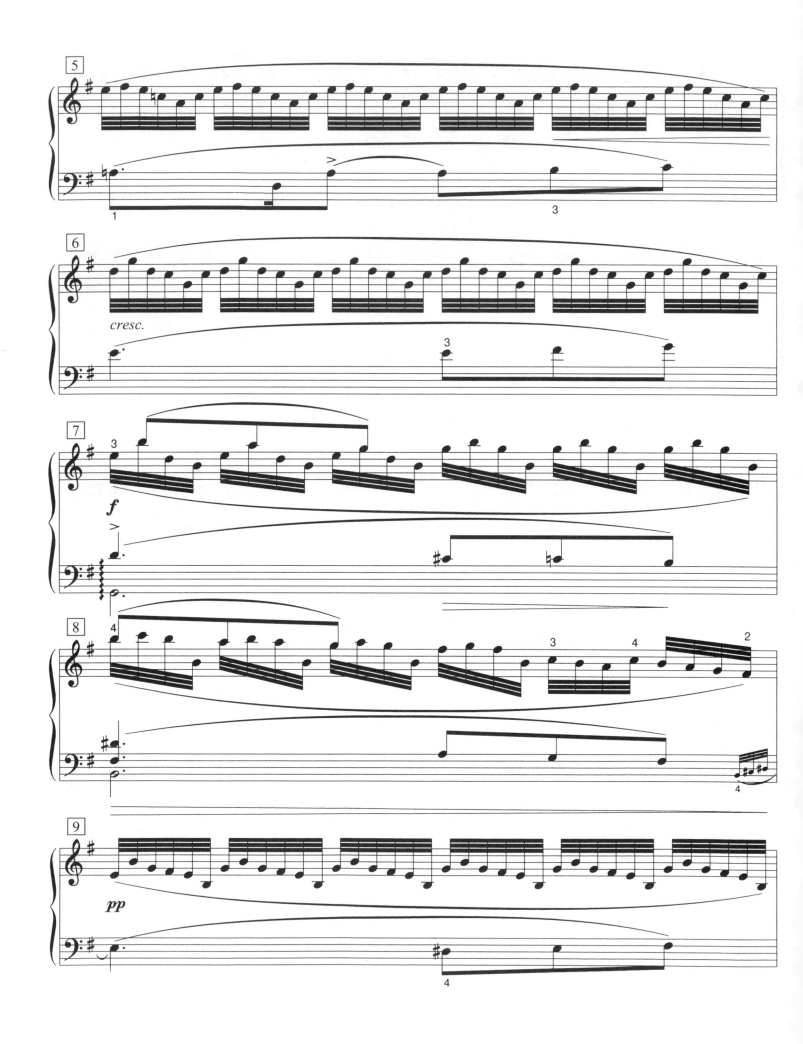

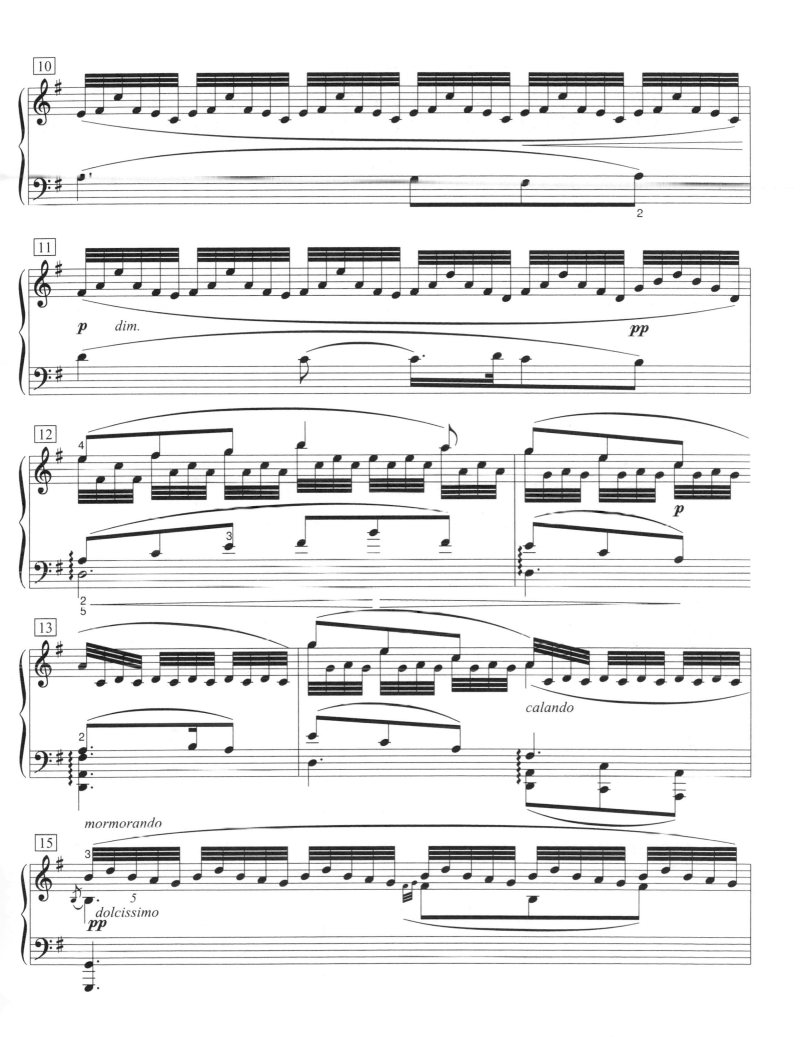

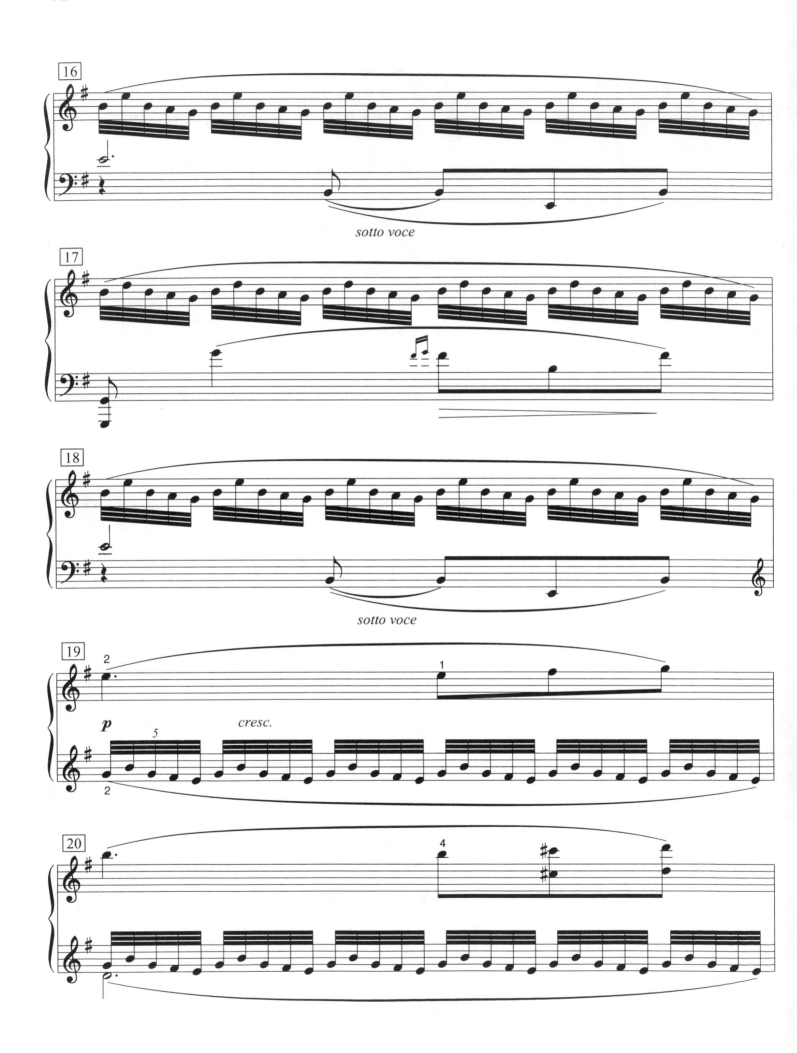

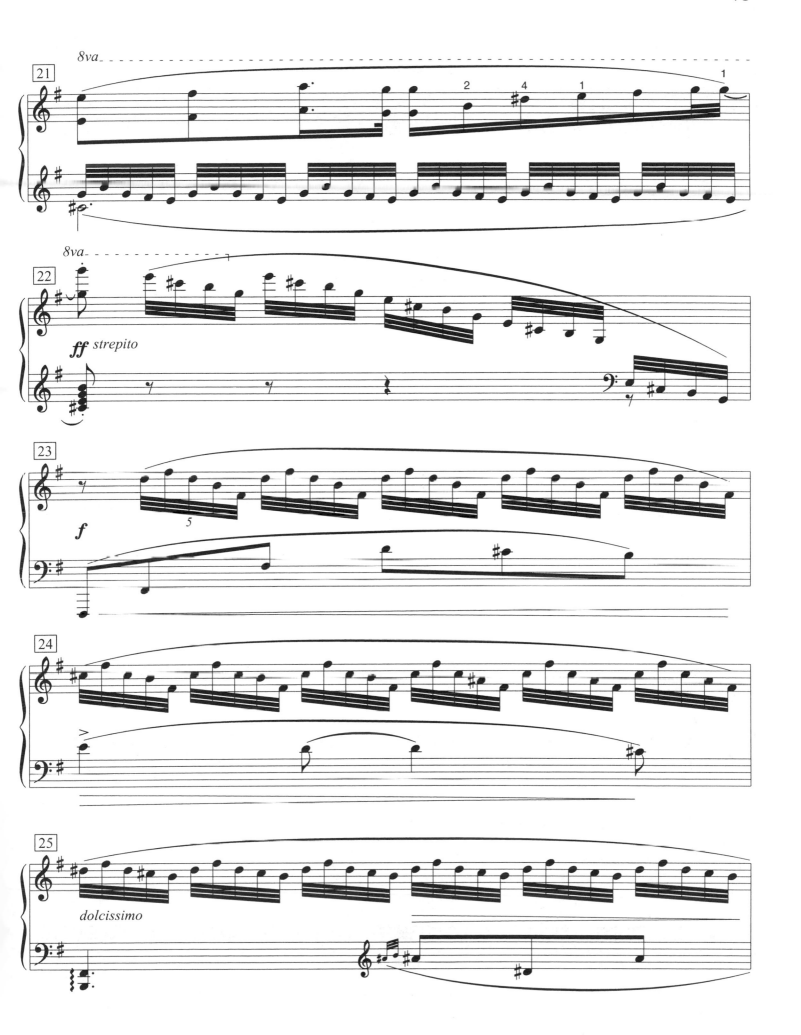

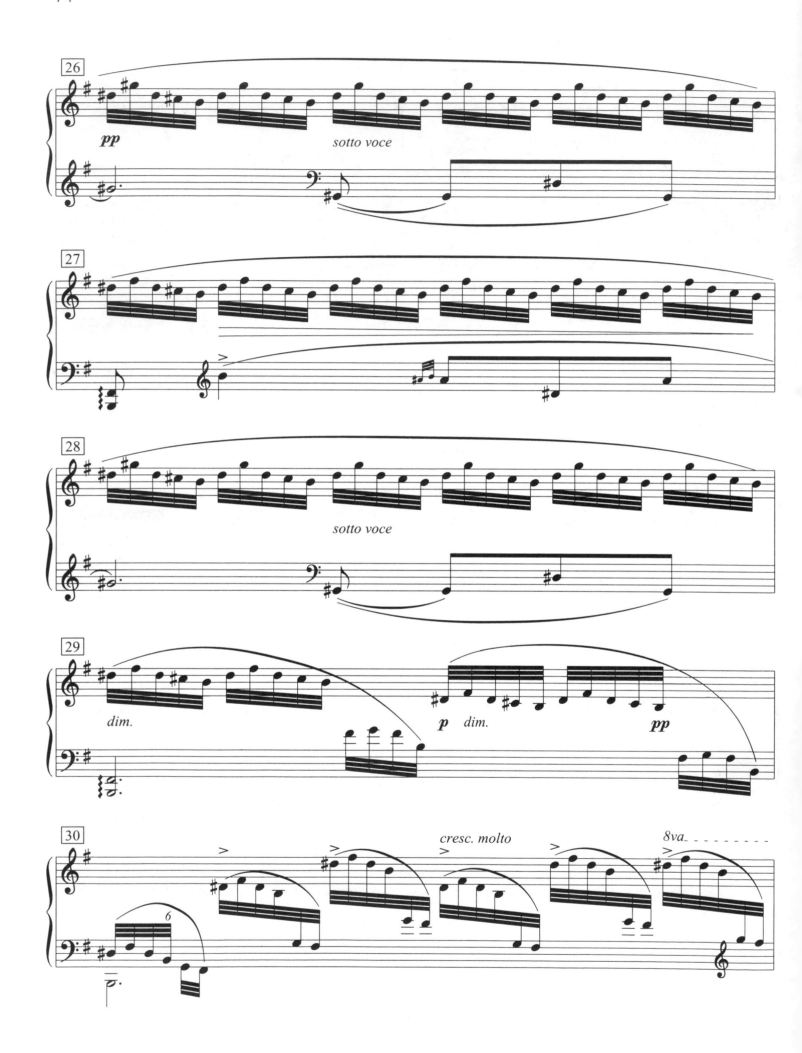

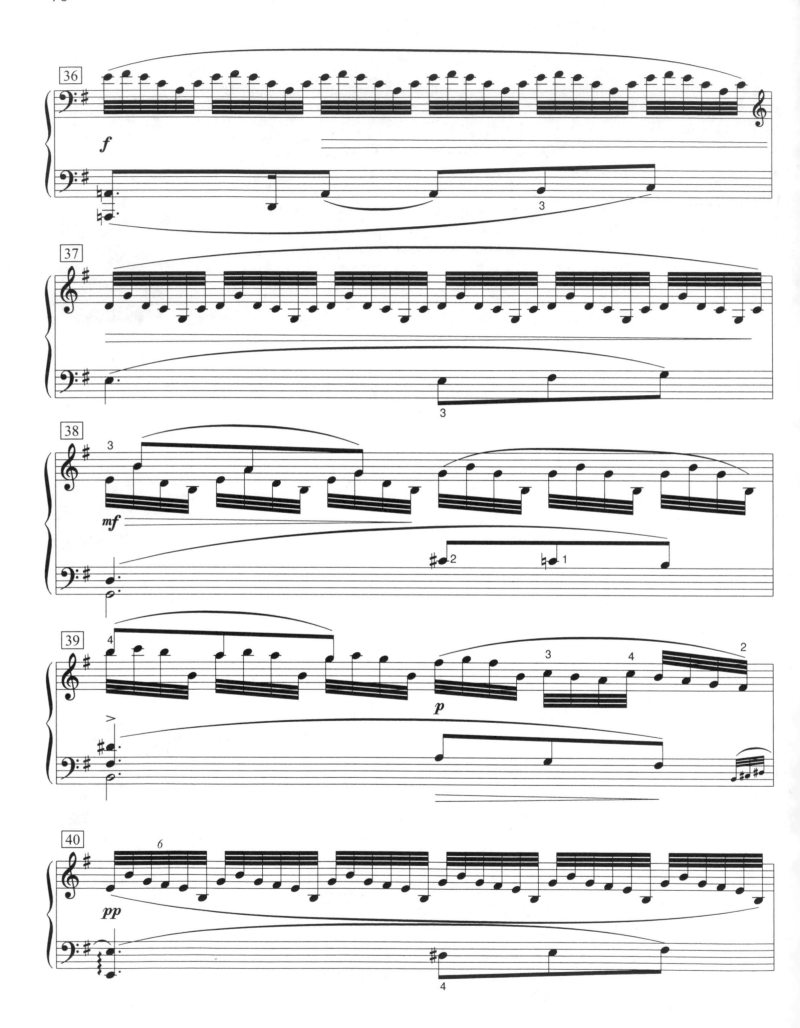

Rhapsody

Op. 11, No. 3

Ernst von Dohnányi
(1877-1960)

The Cat and the Mouse

Scherzo Humoristique

Aaron Copland
(1900 - 1990)

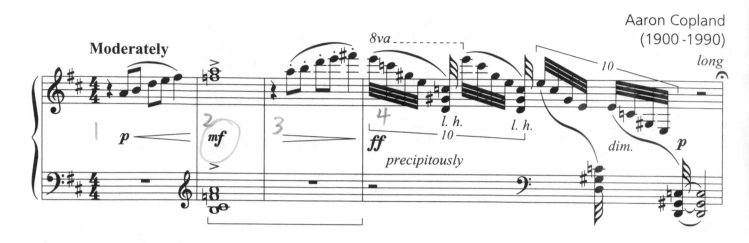

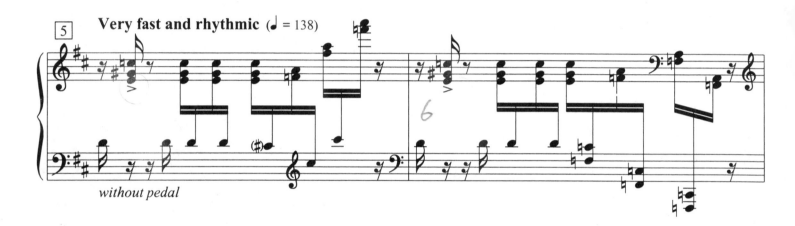

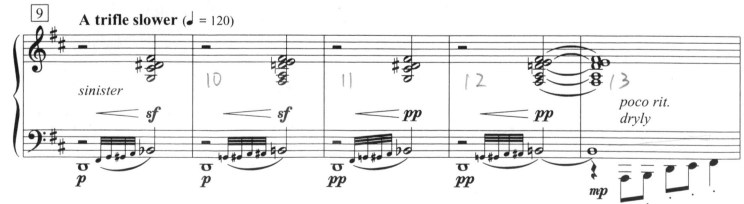

© 1997 Neil A. Kjos Music Company, 4380 Jutland Drive, San Diego, California, 92117.

Toccata

Aram Khachaturian
(1903 -1978)

Allegro marcatissimo

© 1997 Neil A. Kjos Music Company, 4380 Jutland Drive, San Diego, California, 92117.

COMPOSER BIOGRAPHIES

Johannes Brahms (1833-1897), German composer and pianist, received his first music lessons from his father who played double bass in the Hamburg city orchestra. He was a prodigy at the piano and gave his first public performance at the age of ten. In 1853 he made a successful concert tour. At this time he became friends with Liszt and Schumann. Schumann was so impressed with Brahms as a composer that he wrote in his magazine, *Neue Zeitschrift für Music,* "Johannes Brahms is a genius". In 1869 Brahms made Vienna his permanent home and in 1872 became the artistic director of the concerts at Vienna's famous Gesellschaft für Musicfreunde. In 1876 he was given an honorary Doctor of Music degree from Cambridge University, in 1877 he received the Gold Medal of the Philharmonic Society of London, and in 1879 was given an honorary degree of Doctor of Philosophy from the University of Breslau. Brahms was a prolific composer and his works include symphonies, concertos, chamber music, choral and vocal works, and many piano pieces.

Frederic Chopin (1810-1849), born in Poland, lived most of his life in Paris, France. He was a child prodigy at the piano (some say that his talent rivaled that of Mozart). By the time he was twenty, he had already written fifty works for the piano. Chopin was dedicated to writing music for the piano and rarely composed for any other instrument. He wrote over two hundred works for the piano during his lifetime. His piano music is often regarded as the most thoroughly pianistic music ever written.

Aaron Copland (1900-1990), greatly distinguished American composer, lived most of his life in New York. He studied at the American Conservatory in Fontainebleau, near Paris, with Nadia Boulanger. His first published work was *The Cat and the Mouse*, for piano. Other works include ballets, film scores, orchestral music, vocal works, chamber music, and piano pieces. He wrote several books, including *What to Listen for in Music* (1939) and an autobiography, *Copland* (1984).

Claude Debussy (1862-1918), French composer and pianist, entered the Conservatoire Nationale when he was ten years old. At the age of 18, Debussy became the piano teacher for the children of Mme. Nadezhda von Meck, Tchaikovsky's patroness. Debussy traveled with Mme. von Meck's family to Moscow where he became familiar with the music of Borodin and Mussorgsky, which later influenced his compositional style. Other important influences on Debussy's music were his trips to Bayreuth and his introduction to the Javanesse gamelan at the Paris Exposition. Debussy is regarded as the creator of musical Impressionism. He developed a new style of composition which included the use of the oriental pentatonic scale, the whole-tone scale, consecutive parallel chords and intervals, unresolved harmonies and the abandonment of traditional form.

Ernst von Dohnányi (1877-1960), Hungarian pianist, composer, and conductor, studied at the Royal Academy of Music in Budapest. He toured as a pianist throughout Europe and America. He taught piano and composition at the Royal Academy of Music in Budapest and eventually became the director of the Academy. In 1949, he moved to the United States and became composer-in-residence at Florida State University.

Aram Khachaturian (1903-1978), Russian composer, studied 'cello and composition at the Gniessin School in Moscow when his parents moved there from Tiffis when he was seventeen. He graduated from the Moscow Conservatory in 1934 and developed rapidly as a composer writing such frequently played works as the *Piano Concerto*, *Violin Concerto*, *Toccata* (for piano), and the *Sabre Dance* from his ballet *Gayane*.

Anatoli Liadov (1855-1914), Russian composer, was born in St. Petersburg. He studied violin and piano at the St. Petersburg Conservatory and was a composition student of Rimsky-Korsakov. After graduating, Liadov became a professor of theory and composition at the Conservatory. One of his most famous students was Sergei Prokofieff. Liadov wrote numerous piano pieces, choral works, songs and music for orchestra.

Edward MacDowell (1860-1908), American composer, studied in France and Germany. He remained in Germany until 1888 and then returned to America to live in Boston. In 1896 he began teaching at Columbia University for eight years. His mental health began to fail, and he spent the last years of his life unaware of his identity and surroundings. Money was raised for him to live in comfort at Peterborough, New Hampshire. After his death, the residence became a retreat for composers and writers. MacDowell's works include concertos, orchestral works, songs, and many piano pieces.

Felix Mendelssohn (1809-1847), German composer and pianist, first performed in public at the age of nine and began to compose at the age of twelve. He wrote his famous overture to *A Midsummer Night's Dream* when he was seventeen. He traveled extensively to England, Scotland, and the continent. In 1829, Mendelssohn conducted J. S. Bach's *St. Matthew Passion* which was the first performance of a major work by Bach since his death almost eighty years earlier. The result was a revival of interest in Bach's music. Mendelssohn was very busy as a pianist, conductor of orchestras in Düsseldorf and Leipzig, and founder and dean of the Leipzig Conservatory where he taught piano and composition.

Franz Schubert (1797-1828), Austrian composer, began violin lessons when he was eight. He was also given lessons on the piano, organ, composition, and in singing. He followed his father's occupation as a teacher in an elementary school but taught unsuccessfully for three years. During these years he devoted his leisure time to composing songs, and in one year alone (1815) he composed 144 songs. He struggled continually to make a living, although he was recognized as a composer of genius. He was disgracefully underpaid by his publishers, and he lived mostly in extreme poverty. Schubert, who had a great melodic gift, is the acknowledged creator of the Romantic art song (lied), and he wrote over six hundred songs (lieder). He also wrote nine symphonies (including the famous "Unfinished" Symphony), religious works, choral music, operas, chamber music, and numerous piano solo and duet works.

Robert Schumann (1810-1856), German composer and pianist, wrote his first piano pieces when he was seven. In 1832, Schumann injured his hand and began to devote his energies to composition rather than playing the piano. In 1840 he married Clara Wieck, a brilliant pianist who performed many of Schumann's works. Schumann wrote about other musicians as a critic in his magazine, *The New Music Journal*; he was the first to report on the importance of Chopin and Brahms. In 1850 Schumann was appointed Musical Director for the city of Düsseldorf. He held that position until 1853 when mental illness compelled him to resign. His compositions include symphonies, many piano works, a piano concerto, chamber music, songs and choral works.